Tell Me A Story - 1

Adapted by
Swamini Sharda Priyananda
and
Bharati Sukhtankar

Design and Visuals
Nina Bahl

CENTRAL CHINMAYA MISSION TRUST
MUMBAI - 400 072

Published by:
CENTRAL CHINMAYA MISSION TRUST
Sandeepany Sadhanalaya,
Saki Vihar Road,
Mumbai - 400 072, INDIA.
Tel.: 91-22-2857 2367 / 2828 / 5806
Fax: 91-22-2857 3065
E-mail: ccmtpublications@chinmayamission.com
Website: www.chinmayamission.com

Distribution Centre in USA:
CHINMAYA MISSION WEST
Publication Division
560 Bridgetown Pike,
Langhorne, PA 19053, USA.
Tel: (215) 396-0390
Fax: (215) 396-9710
E-mail: publications@chinmaya.org
Website:www.chinmayapublications.org

Design and Visuals
Nina Bahl

Printed by :
JAK Printers Pvt Ltd.

Price : Rs. 125.00

ISBN : 9788175974036

Publisher's Note

CCMT Publications Division has great pleasure in releasing **Tell me a Story I** in its redesigned format adding beautiful visuals to the folk tales. They are specially designed to capture the imagination of our children. The hidden values come alive and talk to us through the imagery. We are thankful to Swamini Shardapriyananda and Bharati Sukhtankar for having initially compiled the stories. We are sure that this book will help children and their parents in imbibing the finer values of life that the stories project.

May 8, 2007   **Central Chinmaya Mission Trust**
Mumbai

CONTENTS

H.H. Swami Chinmayananda
With Bal Vihar Children

Gurudev on Storytelling...

Story telling is an art that should be cultivated by all parents. There is a treasure of joy for the storyteller and a heritage of good that the innocent tiny listener can gain from the story that is told to them. Children can be readily held in attention only by the mesmeric enchantment of the rhythm in the movements of the theme of the story.

While listening to the story a child is in a different mode as children alone can be. They are thrilled by their love for the fantasia. Their imagination lights up and their wide eyed joys are kindled. Children are at such moments in the very lap of Nature gliding on incredible patterns surging in their own hearts.

The very story in the growing child will by itself instill the great truths and higher values of life as time passes on. Tell, never teach a story. Children learn more by a story well told than what we teach them through a story.

EGO DESTROYS

Long, long ago, there lived a king named Satyadharmi. And he was everything his name suggested—good, kind and just. He was also brave and fearless. He always looked after the comforts and needs of his people, protected them from danger, rewarded their good deeds and encouraged all their best efforts. He believed that the law protects those who protect the law –*Dharmo rakshati rakshitah.*

His subjects in turn were extremely loyal, dutiful, hard working and truthful. There was joy and happiness, contentment and peace, throughout the kingdom. Whenever people met, they sang praises of their good king.

One day, the king felt like taking a walk. He walked in the palace gardens and then wandered off into an adjoining jungle. The jungle was cool and beautiful. The king was soon lost in its many charms. After a long time he realised that he was hungry and thirsty. He walked into a nearby ashram. Of the sadhu residing there, he asked, "Tell me, *Maharaj*, which fruits from these trees are to be eaten? Point out to me those which are sweet and juicy and those which are bitter and poisonous so that I may know the difference and eat accordingly."

The sadhu replied, "Friend, you may eat whichever fruit you please. The goodness of

the noble king Satyadharmi is spread all over and you will not find a single bitter or sour fruit anywhere in the kingdom. Long may he live! Why, the bitter neem leaves taste like grapes and the sour tamarind fruit as sweet as a ripe mango — *Dharmo rakshati rakshitah.*"

Satyadharmi ate a handful of neem leaves. Lo! They tasted like big, juicy grapes. He ate the tamarind fruit. It was really as sweet as a ripe mango.

The king was very pleased. He went back to the palace full of good cheer and happy spirits. Alas! He became full of himself. The dangerous little seed of ego was planted in his mind. He started thinking, "I am such a good king. Who in the world can equal my glory? Ha! Ha! Ha! It is the glow of my greatness that you see spread all over."

He no longer cared for his people as he used to. He would spend his time eating, drinking, sleeping, indulging in pleasure and merry sport. The city lost its happy air. People were dismayed. There were quarrels and fights. The crops failed. The rains would not come. And still the king continued his life of pleasure and low thinking.

One day, he set out for a walk. And by chance he wandered into the same jungle as before. After some time he came across the same ashram and the same sadhu. Wanting to hear his own praise again, he thumped the sadhu heartily on the back and said, "Well, my good man. How are things in the forest? Which fruit should I eat this time? The tamarind or the neem? Ha! Ha!"

The holy sadhu frowned with displeasure and said, "The death-knell has sounded! The kingdom is ruined. Everyone is thinking of leaving this kingdom and going to another. The king has become drunk with his own little self. He no longer cares for his people. There is famine and distress everywhere. There are worms in all the fruits. The mango tastes like mud. Life here is no longer worth living— *Dharmo rakshati rakshitah.*"

The expression on the king's face changed. In a trice his pride left him. Hearing the criticism against him opened his eyes. He became humble. He fell at the feet of the sadhu, and said, "I am that wretched sinner, *Maharaj.* I am the unhappy man who has caused all this sorrow. From a good, virtuous king I fell and became wicked and evil. I was swayed by my wretched ego. Bless me, that I may become a good ruler again and that I may never fall back on evil ways as long as I live."

The sadhu blessed him. Satyadharmi went back, a changed man. He tightened his own discipline. He started taking an interest in his kingdom again. Slowly, the gloom lifted. The trees blossomed again. People stopped quarrelling. Crops and fruits were plentiful and sweet. Once again, the king's praises could be heard wherever people paused together in their day's work. *Dharmo rakshati rakshitah !*

THE SCIENCE OF SIGNS

We understand the spoken word if we know the language. We understand the silent gestures if we know the mind of the person making the gestures. In olden days the art of communicating ideas through signs was considered a special science and some pundits used to make a special study of it. It was called *mudra shastra*.

Once a learned king ruled over a kingdom. He encouraged all the arts. Many poets, musicians, artists and pundits adorned his royal court. The king became very famous because of the learned discourses and discussions that were frequently held in his court.

In a neighbouring country there lived a pundit who specialised in *mudra shastra*. Holding discussions with several others who had studied this science, he defeated them all. Everyone was afraid to face him in debate because no one could win over him. One day, the *mudra pundit* sent word to the king that he would visit his court on a certain day to hold discussions on *mudra shastra* with the pundits of the royal court. If they succeeded, he would surrender all his titles to them and leave. Otherwise the king and his pundits should acknowledge him as the greatest pundit.

Now, in the king's court pundits in all branches of literature were available, but there was not a single one in *mudra shastra*. The king was worried. He did not want to acknowledge defeat because the royal court had won great reputation before, which he did not want to lose. So he held a conference of all the pundits in his court to think of a way out of the dilemma.

Everyone was worried and no one knew what to do. At last one shrewd pundit suggested, "Rajan, try as we may, we cannot face the *mudra pundit* in debate and win. So let us try to defeat him by a trick. We will dress up one shrewd man in our kingdom as a pundit and invite the *mudra pundit* to hold discussions with him. Who knows, by his shrewdness our man may win the debate. We don't stand to lose anything, even if he is defeated."

Everyone approved of the suggestion, and the king also agreed to take the chance. An old, clever shepherd was selected for the purpose. He was finely dressed up as a pundit. His tall, erect figure lent much to his dignity.

When the *mudra pundit* reached the court he was received with due honours and was introduced to the make-believe pundit. The king said, "O wise man, please have your discussions with our pundit. We are willing to abide by your conditions. If you win, we will acclaim you as the best; if he wins, you will have to surrender all your titles to him."

The two pundits sat face to face and commenced the discussions. The king and others eagerly looked on.

The *mudra pundit* raised his hand and showed one finger. The shepherd was a one-eyed man. He stared hard with his one eye for some time, and slowly raised his hand and showed two fingers.

There was an appreciative smile on the face of the *mudra pundit*. He then raised his hand

once again and showed three fingers. The shepherd did not hesitate this time. He closed all his fingers and showed his fist.

The *mudra pundit* immediately rose and fell at the feet of the shepherd in great respect. Then he surrendered his titles to him, loudly acclaiming the old pundit's wisdom and scholarship. He took leave of the king and left the court. The whole court was astounded. They could not follow anything at all. The real pundits of the court followed the *mudra pundit* as he was leaving, and asked him out of curiosity, "Sir, may we know what the discussions were about? We could not follow because we do not know the science. So, please explain."

The *mudra pundit* was still in ecstasy. He again praised the great wisdom of the royal pundit and said. "Ah, what a pundit! I have never before seen such an expert in the science, nor such a philosopher."

"First of all, I showed one finger to say that God is one. Your pundit replied with his two fingers, indicating that there are two... *jeevatma* and *parmatma*. I then said with my three fingers, that *jeevatma*, *parmatma* and *Ishwara* are three."

"The wise pundit of the court closed all his fingers and showed his fist, thus pointing out that all the three are really one. Ah, great indeed, is his wisdom!"

The pundits revelled in this description. Taking leave of the *mudra pundit*, they returned to the court and related to the king what they had heard. They wanted to know what the shepherd had understood of the discussions. The shepherd was very pleased with his performance, for he had upheld the reputation of the court and was also richly rewarded by the king. So, when he was asked what discussions he had with the *mudra pundit*, he replied in high spirits.

"My dear Sirs, your *mudra pundit* was very rude and insulting, but actually, he was a coward. First he raised one finger, mocking at me for having only one eye. I crisply retorted with two fingers that my one was much better than his two eyes."

"But he didn't stop at this. He again insulted me, showing three fingers to point out that together ours were three eyes. I really got angry at his rudeness and showed him my fist, indicating that I would break his nose if he further insulted me. Then the coward was afraid and fell at my feet." The king and his pundits split their sides with laughter over this. They realised their good fortune in getting such a pundit for the discussions.

THE ADVICE

There once lived a king who was extremely fond of shikar. One day, he was out in the jungle with his ministers and servants. He was in search of daring adventure, longing to come face-to-face with a wild elephant or a man-eating tiger.

When they were hunting, they came across a sadhu who kept repeating —

"My advice will be sold
For one hundred *mohurs* of gold!
Jai Jagadeesha Hare!
Jai Jai Jagadeesha Hare!"

Now, the king was a good sport. He was willing to try anything once. He thought, "What is a hundred gold *mohurs* to me! And if his advice is really worth it, why then, I shall be a better man!"

So, he went to the sadhu and giving him the gold said, "*Maharaj*, please give me this advice you spoke of."

The sadhu calmly took the *mohurs* and said, "O king, always remember this—never do anything before thinking of what its effects will be." It was a 'Look-before-you-leap' advice.

Now the king's minister laughed and thought, "Ha! Such an ordinary thing, and the cost is a hundred gold *mohurs*! What a fool the king is!"

The king knew the minister's mind very well. Nevertheless, with perfect gravity he said to him, "See that the Mahatma's words are engraved on stone and placed in the palace so that I can always see them."

"Jai Jagadeesha Hare!
Jai Jai Jagadeesha Hare!"

The minister was now quite sure that his king was a little weak mentally. But he thought, "I might as well humour him," and he went to carry out the king's bidding.

A short time later, one of the king's enemies met the royal *vaidya* and said to him, "If you are successful in poisoning the king, I will give you five thousand gold *mohurs*." The physician was not a very rich man. Besides, he had a greedy wife and a large number of children to support. And then, five thousand gold *mohurs* was a large sum of money, indeed! So he agreed to this disloyal scheme.

After a few days, as chance would have it, the king developed a fever. It was too good a chance for the physician to miss. With extreme satisfaction, thinking greedily of his five thousand gold *mohurs*, he mixed a potion of poison for the royal patient. He was about to give it to the king. But suddenly his eyes fell on the words engraved in stone—the valuable 'Look-before-you-leap' advice. This set the *vaidya* thinking, "If the king dies after taking poison, the courtiers will surely cut me to pieces. Of what use then will five thousand gold *mohurs* be to me?"

So he threw away the poison and mixed another potion for the king—this time the true medicine.

"Jai Jagadeesha Hare!
Jai Jai Jagadeesha Hare!"

Now the king was a very clever and alert man. He had noticed every movement of the *vaidya*. So he asked, "O doctor, tell me the truth. Why did you throw away the first medicine and mix a second one for me? If you do not give me a true answer, you will be executed." The *vaidya* trembled with fear and spilled the whole plot. But since he had been sincere, the king granted

him pardon. The enemy, however, was tracked down and put to death.

The king then sent for his minister and said, "The other day you had laughed at the sadhu's advice. But you can see how useful it has proved to be. Had the *vaidya* really given me the poison, I would have died, and the *vaidya* would have been killed. There would have been riots. The kingdom would have been in chaos and confusion."

The minister had no answer. He hung his head in shame.

"Jai Jagadeesha Hare !
Jai Jai Jagadeesha Hare !"

THE ONE PROTECTOR

The construction work was in progress. Huge rocks and stones loaded on to creaking carts were being dragged up the hill where the fort was being built. The sun was high. It was almost noon. The backs of the labourers glistened with sweat and perspiration trickled down their brows.

Shivaji, king of the Marathas stood there supervising the work. He made a fine figure, straight and majestic with his arms akimbo. He was not very tall. He had a pointed beard, a straight nose and bright eyes. His sardars ran hither and thither carrying out his orders. Another great Maratha fort was being built!

In this bustle of activity was suddenly heard a rich, powerful voice, *"Jai Jai Raghuveera Samartha."* Before Shivaji stood a sadhu. He had a staff and begging bowl in his hand and wore only a saffron coloured loin-cloth. Shivaji bowed his head and folding his hands, asked for the mendicant's blessing. *"Jai Jai Raghuveera Samartha."* His name was Ramdas Swami!

Then Shivaji drew him into conversation. Ramdas said, "What is this you are doing Shivaji? You seem very busy today!" Shivaji said,

"O, what shall I tell you Swamiji! Wearing a monarch's crown is no joke. I have so many responsibilities. I have to feed and clothe my people. I have to build these forts to guard against Mughal invasions."

"Which other king has achieved so much in so short a time? I started only with a small group of faithful Mavlis. Now I have built up a mighty empire—the only empire which has defied the Mughal empire!"

Shivaji's chest swelled with pride. He felt at the peak of his glory as he told the smiling Swami the list of his achievements. Soon, it was noon. Shivaji invited Ramdas Swami for *bhiksha*. They made their way to the palace.

The Swami was received with proper honours. *"Jai Jai Raghuveera Samartha"*. He was served the choicest of dishes by the queen herself. And all the time the Swami was thinking, "Shivaji is a very good king, no doubt. But he has become proud. Pride has been the downfall of many a good man. If he is not taught a lesson now, the Maratha empire will lose all that it has gained. Shivaji must be made to realise and see the hand of God working through him, and his men." Outwardly, Ramdas Swami smiled. He blessed the queen and praised the king. "*Jai Jai Raghuveera Samartha*."

The meal over, Shivaji and Ramdas went back to the site of the fort. The building work had been resumed. Some men dragged the blocks of stone up the hill, some carried up the water, some urged on the oxen, some sat and hammered the huge stones to a smaller size.

Shivaji was trying to show his own importance by scolding his men, urging them to work harder. At the place where the monarch and the mendicant were standing, some men were breaking stones. They watched them with interest. Suddenly, one stone cracked and a frog hopped out. *"Jai Jai Raghuveera Samartha."*

"Look at that, Shivaji," said Ramdas. "Probably it is due to your mercy that the poor frog managed to survive in that stone. How your glory has spread in the land! You are indeed the greatest king on earth!" And the Swami gave a low, chuckling laugh. *"Jai Jai Raghuveera Samartha."*

Now Shivaji was a very shrewd and clever man. He understood at once what Swami Ramdas was trying to teach him. Understanding came into his intelligent eyes. He clasped the feet of the sadhu and said, *"Maharaj*, forgive me. I have been vain. I have been drawing to myself the glory that belongs to God. I will never let vain thoughts enter my mind again. *"Jai Jai Raghuveera Samartha."*

That was a golden moment in history. Shivaji surrendered himself completely to Ramdas Swami. Thenceforward he became Shivaji's *Rajguru*—always guiding and correcting him, ever putting him on the right path. He put Shivaji under an oath that he would not rest till he had unfurled the saffron-coloured flag of the Hindu religion on every fort he came across. It was the first step in the mighty movement of Hindu revival under the oppression of Mughal rule.

Shivaji never forgot his Guru's loving words, "Who was it, Shiva, that put water in the coconut? Who put milk in the breast of flesh and blood? Remember, all this glory and wonder is His. All His! *Jai Jai Raghuveera Samartha.*"

And throughout his life Shivaji served but one goal—the revival of his eternal mother—the Hindu religion! "*Jai Jai Raghuveera Samartha.*"

THE TRUE DEVOTEE

Lord Shiva once had a *bhakta,* who was a king, rich and powerful. Every year he would worship at the shrine of Shiva, and the occasion would turn out to be a big festival. People would throng the streets like holiday-makers. Brahmins would flock from all parts of the country. The king would distribute rich gifts among them. The poor would gather for free food and clothing. Thus the king would spend lavishly each year, performing elaborate ceremonies to worship Lord Shiva.

"Sambho Mahadeva Deva,
Shiva Sambho Mahadeva Devesa Sambho,
Sambho Mahadeva Deva."

After one such worship was over, the king went to his palace to rest. He was completely satisfied with himself. Was he not a great devotee of Lord Shiva? Had he not spent great wealth for the worship? Had he not acquired great merit by distributing food and clothing, gold and gifts, horses and cows? Had he not fed and clothed the poor? Could Lord Shiva ever hope to have a greater devotee on this earth?

The king, thinking of his own greatness and goodness, soon fell asleep.

As he slept, he had a dream. In the dream, Lord Shiva appeared to him and said, "O king, you are not a true devotee. You are proud and vain of your achievements. I do not recognise your worship at all. Such show and pomp do not please me. If you want to see a true devotee of mine, go to the edge of the forest. There lives a poor woodcutter. He is my real *bhakta*."

"Sambho Mahadeva Deva,
Shiva Sambho Mahadeva Devesa Sambho,
Sambho Mahadeva Deva."

The king woke up, vexed and angry. A mere woodcutter! A greater *bhakta* than he, a mighty king! Was it possible?

He set out alone, early in the morning, till he reached the outskirts of the forest. There he saw a little mud hut. A bare-backed woodcutter was setting out into the forest with an axe on his shoulder. The king stopped him and asked, "How do you worship Lord Shiva?" The woodcutter folded his palms humbly and said, "I am but a poor woodcutter. I earn two coins a day. One coin I spend on my food. One-fourth of the rest I give in charity, and three quarters I save. On Monday, I offer Lord Shiva a little kheer made of broken rice. When I cut wood, I chant the Lord's name the whole day. I know nothing other than Shiva."

"*Sambho Mahadeva Deva,*
Shiva Sambho Mahadeva Devesa Sambho,
Sambho Mahadeva Deva."

The king at once felt the love and humility of this simple worship. He went back to the palace, chanting "Shiva, Shiva", his heart purified by the darshan of the Lord's true *bhakta*.

DO IT TODAY

In the hills of North India, there once lived a Mahatma, Sadananda by name. Word of his powers and miracles had spread far and wide. Many people would come from far-off places to visit him. Among them was a devotee, Sri Tamasapriya, who became extremely attached to the service of the master. He would run errands, cook the meals, clean the room and look after all the physical needs of the Mahatma.

After many months of such dedicated service, the Mahatma called him one day and said, "My son, I am going away from this place. Here is a magic stone. Any iron object you touch with it will immediately turn into gold. I am giving you this as a reward for all your service to me. But I will come back after two days and take back the stone. So you have two days to make yourself rich for the rest of your life." Tamasapriya bowed his head in gratitude and the Mahatma left.

When the Mahatma had gone, Tamasapriya thought to himself, "I have got two days to make all the gold I want. Today I will rest after all the hard work I have done. Tomorrow

morning I will go and get a mound of iron and convert it into gold." So saying he went to sleep and got up towards noon the next day. Immediately he went to the marketplace. The iron-monger's shop had closed for the afternoon, so he decided to have a good meal at a cheap hotel. After the meal he felt drowsy and lay down under a shady banyan tree. By the time he woke up, the sun had set, the shops had closed, and the people were heading home. So he too started wending his way home, consoling himself that he still had a day at his disposal.

Next morning he got up early and went to the iron-monger's shop. The iron-monger weighed him a mound of iron, but the problem was how to get it home. He sought the help of some people, but it being a busy market day they all had their own work to do. So he decided to go home and get his brothers to help him with his load. Now, the marketplace was quite a distance from his house. The afternoon sun shone fiercely overhead, so Tamasapriya rested for some time under a shady tree. Refreshed after his rest, he continued on his journey home and reached at sundown.

Imagine his dismay when he saw the quiet figure of the Mahatma on his doorstep! The man fell at his feet and begged for the stone, for another day. The Mahatma just smiled and said, "O fool, why did you go so far to get iron? Why did you not convert the iron objects in your own home to gold? What, not even the latch on the door have you touched!"

Opportunities not availed are, indeed, opportunities lost! Never be a Tamasapriya, a lover of indolence.

THE FIRE TOUCH

Way up in the Himalayas, where the snow never melts, there once sat a *rakshasa* performing severe penance. He was a devotee of Lord Shiva and had spent many, many hundreds of years, with no thought of food or clothes, heat or cold, sun or snow, sitting there, his mind fixed on Lord Shiva. "*Shiva-Shiva-Shiva-Shiva-Shiva.*" His name was Bhasmasura.

After ages had passed thus, Shiva decided to bless him. So, one day, as Bhasmasura was meditating, the Lord appeared before him. He was shining like the morning sun. He was the supreme ascetic, dressed in deer skin, body smeared with ashes, locks matted, the snakes dangling around his neck and arms, his hand holding aloft the divine *trishul*. Ah, what a magnificent sight he made in all his ascetic glory! Bhasmasura's eyes were dazzled. He was speechless with wonder at the Lord's beautiful form, "*Shiva-Shiva-Shiva-Shiva-Shiva.*"

Gently Shiva spoke to the awe-struck Bhasmasura. He said, "I am pleased with the severe penance you have performed. Ask of me any boon you desire." And Bhasmasura thought, "I must indeed be a great *tapasvi*, as Lord Shiva has granted me a boon." Aloud he said, "Lord, grant that whatever object I touch with my right hand should immediately be reduced to ashes, *Shiva-Shiva.*" Bhasmasura, even after going through such rigorous penance, had an *asuric* mind. "*Shiva-Shiva.*" What a boon to ask! Lord Shiva said, "*Tathaastu!* So be it."

At once Bhasmasura said, "Lord, you have granted me the boon alright, but how will I know if it is true? Once you disappear, I will not be able to see you perhaps for the next few hundred years. I would like to test your boon. This is a mountainous, snowy area. For miles around there is no object that can be touched. Therefore, come forward. I will touch your head and see if what you say is true."

"Shiva-Shiva-Shiva-Shiva-Shiva."

The wicked *rakshasa* thought that once he burnt Lord Shiva to ashes there would be nobody greater than him.

Panic rose in Shiva's heart. He knew that if he complied with Bhasmasura's request he would

surely turn to ashes. And if he was no more, the world would come to a chaotic end. Yet, once having granted a boon, how could he take it back? There was only one way out of this sticky situation—he would have to run!

And run he did. Clutching his trident, he ran as fast as his legs would carry him. He ran over mountains and down valleys, he crossed rivers and lakes, he ran across vast plains and fields, he passed peaceful ashrams and huts, he ran

through dark, dense forests and light, cheerful woods—with Bhasmasura never far behind! "*Shiva-Shiva-Shiva-Shiva-Shiva.*"

What a strange sight it was! The Lord of the Universe running for his life pursued by an evil-minded *rakshasa!* The hearts of the birds fluttered as they twittered from the treetops. The animals stared with huge startled eyes as they scampered out of the way. And the chase went on—Shiva, panic-stricken, panting ahead; Bhasmasura, thirsting to test his unintelligent boon, close on his heels!

Shiva was now getting out of breath. The chase had been long and tiring. Yet, what could he do? He had to press on. But he was beginning to feel that unless something happened soon, Bhasmasura would have his way.

At this time Vishnu was in *Vaikuntha*, watching this unusual occurence with amused interest. He thought that Shiva had been sufficiently punished for carelessly granting such a boon. It was time now to go and help him. After all, were they not the very best of friends? "*Shiva-Shiva-Shiva-Shiva-Shiva.*"

Shiva had just turned round the shoulder of a mountain and Bhasmasura had not yet reached the bend. Vishnu transformed himself into a delightful maiden, soft, shy and beautiful and stood at the bend. As Bhasmasura came panting up, hot in Shiva's pursuit, Mohini, the girl gently caught his hand and said, "Maharaj! you look very tired indeed. Why are you running so fast? Come, my father's ashram is not far away. Come and rest awhile there. Take some refreshment. Then you can start with renewed vigour."

Bhasmasura shook off her hand impatiently and said, "O, let me go. That wretched Shiva will get away. I want to touch his head with my right hand so he will be burnt to ashes and I can then become Lord of the three worlds."

He was about to run ahead when he saw Mohini properly for the first time. The image soon filled his eyes. Her lovely black tresses, her smooth fair brow, her large, soft, doe-like eyes and her small delicate mouth. He looked at the shapely wrist and fingers resting lightly on his arm, her lissome body, her fair feet with tinkling anklets and he forgot all about Shiva and his boon. He looked Mohini up and down, not once, not twice, but over and over again. Desire was planted in his heart. *"Shiva-Shiva-Shiva-Shiva-Shiva."*

He lunged forward to catch her, but Mohini quickly stepped back. Then Bhasmasura said, "You are so very beautiful, Mohini. I want you to be my bride. Will you marry me?"

Mohini gave a rippling little laugh. She said, "Maharaj, how can I trust you? The man I marry must never have another wife. Once he marries me, he should never marry again. But you *rakshasas* have many, many wives. No, it cannot be." Saying this, she let out a long, wistful sigh.

Bhasmasura, now crazy with desire said, "Mohini, I cross my heart I shall not marry again. I promise you that if you become my wife I will not look at another woman. Please, please give your consent to marry me."

Mohini looked at Bhasmasura and then looked modestly away. "O, you men. I know you are all the same. *Shiva-Shiva.* None of you is to be trusted. Promises! Promises! But you never stick to them. No, I shall not be satisfied till you place your hand on your head and swear that you will not marry again if I become your wife."

Bhasmasura now thoroughly caught up in this net of *maya*, quickly touched his head with his right hand. "Mohini, I swear..." he began. But he never lived even to complete his sentence. For, the moment he placed his hand on his head, he was burnt to a heap of ashes. "*Shiva-Shiva-Shiva-Shiva-Shiva.*"

Shiva was still heaving and panting as he ran along. He looked nervously over his shoulder to see how close Bhasmasura was to him. But for quite a distance behind he saw no Bhasmasura. Strange! What could have happened? He could not have sat down to rest. He had tremendous energy and did not tire easily. For some time Shiva waited where he was. But still there was no sign of Bhasmasura.

So, he retraced his steps and reached that very bend. He saw there a huge heap of ashes and the most beautiful girl, standing there next to it. He asked her if she knew what had happened to Bhasmasura. Very modestly, she narrated all that had happened.

Shiva was very pleased with her timely assistance. Above all, he was pleased at the way she praised him, "Lord, I saw you running and sensed your distress. I saw you were in need of help. Had Bhasmasura caught up with you and placed his hand on your head, where would the poor creatures of this earth have been? Therefore, I tricked him into placing his hand on his own head by asking him to swear that he would never marry anyone else if I agreed to marry him. I did this all for your sake, my Lord." Thus saying she folded her hands and bowed her head.

Shiva beamed. He made to embrace her. But she slipped from his arms. Bewildered he looked around. There was no sign of Mohini anywhere. Instead, there stood the beautiful resplendent form of the four-armed Lord Vishnu. The corners of His mouth lifted in a slow smile.

Shiva smiled too, as he realised that once again the Supreme Protector of the Universe had run to the aid of the good and manoeuvred the destruction of the evil.

"Shiva-Shiva-Shiva-Shiva-Shiva."

WE ARE ONE

Up in the Himalayas, away from the world, tucked away in the lap of the holy mountains, on the banks of sacred rivers, lived holy men. They spent their days lost in meditation. They lived in simple huts – *kutias*. To a holy mind, these *kutias* were very beautiful – untouched by the noisy dust of the city. They had a natural abundance of flowers and fruits, animals and birds, trees and creepers, bees and honey.

In one of these ashrams lived a Mahatma, Swami Sivoham, with a few disciples. He was known to teach his students in a practical way. Once he demonstrated a great truth to them, they could never forget their lesson.

Swami Sivoham wanted to explain to them that one being is not separate from another, if only one recognises that the same Lord resides in each of us.

But his disciples, not having understood fully the teaching of the lesson, would at times indulge in petty quarrels.

So the Mahatma decided it was time to teach them, by his own special technique. Then they would never forget! He told the disciples, "Tomorrow, children, I shall arrange a big feast for you. I shall expect all of you to partake of the food I prepare for you."

The next day, all his disciples gathered for the promised meal. He made them sit in two rows, one facing the other. Then he himself served them the delicious dishes he had prepared. There were all kinds of rich and spicy foods, and a number of tasty sweets. The poor students, who up to then had been eating only what the forest could give them, were quite happily surprised to see the mouth-watering food before them. They could not wait to start.

Just as they were about to take the first morsel to their mouths, their Guru called out, "Wait, wait! Don't start eating yet. Just wait for a few moments." Thus saying, he got a few planks of wood. Then, straightening the right hand of each disciple, he tied a plank of wood to it, with the result that the right arms of all the students became stiff. Then he said, "Eat now, my children. Eat as much as you can." The disciples

looked at each other in dismay. How could they eat with their arms stiffened by wood? How could they take the food to their mouths?

The Mahatma saw their confusion and laughed gently. "Dear ones," he said, "is it really necessary that each of you should put the food in his own mouth? For a change, why do you not feed the person in front of you?"

So the disciples, after the initial embarrassment, fed each other. They clasped the feet of their Guru, who gave them their lessons so lovingly. Yes, "all hands are His... all mouths are His". Every hand can serve all mouths if only willing! *"Parabrahma Nityam Tadevaahamasmi*—That Eternal Supreme *Brahman* am I."

DIGESTING A GIANT

Long, long ago, our country was full of forests, and the cities and villages were few. It was a great risk for people to travel from one place to another, as they had to pass through thick forests which were inhabited by cruel giants and wild animals.

In the forests of South India there lived two big giants, Vaataapi and Ilwala, who were brothers. They were both cannibals and killed human beings whenever they got an opportunity. Their method of killing their victims was unique.

Ilwala, disguised as a pious Brahmin, would approach the travellers who passed by, with a humble request that they should come over to his house to rest and be his guest for a day. The innocent travellers readily accepted his invitation, for it was difficult to travel or get food in a jungle. Ilwala led them courteously to his house, requesting them to take a bath and rest. He retired into the kitchen to cook food. There he killed his own brother Vaataapi and cutting him to pieces, cooked tasty dishes with his flesh. When the meal was ready, he approached the guests, and served them the meals.

The guests, who did not know what the dishes were, enjoyed the food. As they finished and were about to get up, Ilwala stood before them and called out, "Vaataapi, Vaataapi, come, come out." Hearing this call, Vaataapi, in the form of meat in the stomachs of the guests, became alive and, tearing the guests into pieces, emerged out of them. Thereafter the brothers enjoyed the sumptuous meal consisting of the flesh of the guests.

And so the innocent, unsuspecting guests fell into their snare. This terrible secret somehow leaked out, and the sages living in the forests approached Maharshi Agastya requesting him to end the demoniac ways of the giants. Agastya replied *"Hari Om, Hari Om."*

So Maharshi Agastya agreed to vanquish the terrible giants Vaataapi and Illwala, and started for the place where they lived, *"Hari Om, Hari Om."*

Ilwala, always on the lookout for victims, espied the Maharshi and came towards him disguised as a Brahmin in the usual way. He respectfully requested the Maharshi to be his guest and sanctify his house. Agastya, chanting *"Hari Om, Hari Om,"* readily agreed. As soon as they reached the house, Ilwala joined his palms in mock humility and said, "Mahatma, please take your bath and do your *japa, Hari Om, Hari Om*. In the meanwhile I will prepare the meal."

Thus leaving the Maharshi in the front room, he went in and prepared the usual meal with Vaataapi's flesh. As noon time neared, he approached the Mahrshi and humbly requested him to come into the dining room to partake of the meal.

The food was served with great care. Agastya enjoyed the meal very much, *"Hari Om."* The dishes were tasty and he very well knew what he was eating. As soon as the meal was over, passing his left hand over his stomach again and again, he muttered slowly, *"Hari Om, Hari Om,* be digested Vaataapi, *Hari Om,* be digested." Ilwala could not hear what the Maharshi was saying, as it was said in a very low tone. He was completely absorbed in the thoughts of the delicious meal he and his brother would have together, for the Mahrshi looked quite hefty. His meat was bound to be very delicious.

Immersed in his thoughts he was only waiting for the Maharshi to finish the meal. As Agastya finished eating and was washing his hands, *"Hari Om, Hari Om,"* Ilwalla stood before him and called out aloud, "Vaataapi, O Vaataapi, come, come out." A few moments passed but nothing happened. Ilwala was puzzled at the delay in the appearance of Vaataapi. Agastya looked at Ilwala, *"Hari Om, Hari Om,"* and smiled. "Which Vaataapi are you referring to? Your brother has been already digested. *Hari Om, Hari Om."*

Ilwala was terrified. He knew by now that in front of him was an extraordinary sage with divine powers whom he could not harm. Surely the sage could reduce him to ashes with one look from his eyes. Trembling he fell at the feet of the Maharshi and begged, "Mahatma, please spare my life. I will not commit such a sin again." Agastya took pity on him and said, "Alright, this time I will leave you. Go away from this forest, and live elsewhere. Even there you won't be safe from me if you repeat this again. Stop all killing. If I hear of a single case of killing by you, know that it will be the end of you. *Hari Om, Hari Om."*

Ilwala solemnly swore not to kill anyone again. He left the forest as he was told and went away to live elsewhere.

THE FOOLISH LION

In a certain jungle lived a lion. He was very powerful and very strong, as most lions are. He would freely roam in the forest . Whenever he found a healthy looking animal—a grazing buffalo, a tender hare or a timid deer, he would pounce upon it, tear it to pieces and make a tasty meal of it.

One day, it so happened that he roamed and roamed about, but could not find a single animal. Whenever the animals heard his echoing roar, they trembled and scurried to their little hideouts.

The sun had set. Dusk and darkness descended upon the jungle. The lion, tired after his fruitless search, came upon a cave. An idea struck him. It was dark now and the animal living in that cave would soon be coming home.

So he decided he would wait, and when the animal came he would eat it up. He hid in a dark corner of the cave and waited.

After some time a fox came there. The cave was his home. But foxes, as you know, are very cunning. He saw pug marks leading to his cave, but not coming out of it. And the pug marks looked like those of a lion. So the fox decided to be sure before he entered the cave. But how could he know, unless he entered the cave? After much thought, he hit upon an idea. He called out, "Hello there, cave, dear friend." The lion got excited when he heard the voice of an animal call. Ah! Now it would not be very long before he would have his long-awaited meal. His pangs of hunger grew sharper and his mouth watered! He did not say anything. He waited.

The fox, getting no answer, called out again, "My dear cave. Have you forgotten our agreement to greet each other whenever I leave or enter you? Or is it that there is a wild animal hiding in you, and you are not answering out of fear?"

The lion thought, "Better not leave room for suspicion. Maybe the cave is not answering because I am in it. Better answer and remove all doubts." So, he called back, "O, hello, friend. I did not answer you before because I was thinking of something else. Do come in."

The fox waiting outside was now satisfied. He slipped away slyly, chuckling to himself, his eyes twinkling with mischief. He had hoodwinked the lion and saved his own neck!

SRI RAMA JAYAM

There is a time to laugh and a time to weep. There is a time to smile and a time to be serious. Things have to be done at the proper time and place, only then are they appreciated. At other times they are misunderstood and create a lot of trouble. This happened even to the mighty Lakshmana, who was the brother of Sri Rama and his greatest devotee.

At the behest of his father, Sri Rama had to renounce the kingdom and go to the forests for fourteen years. His beloved wife Sita and loving brother Lakshmana followed him, as they could not bear to be away from him. *Sri Rama Jayam* was Lakshmana's aim and motto in life.

In the forest Lakshmana took it upon himself to serve his brother and his sister-in-law just as the eyelid does an eye. During the day he gathered fruits and roots for their food, provided water for their bath, etc. During the nights he sat outside their *parnasala* with his bow and arrows, to protect them from demons and cruel animals that were prowling about. Thus he was on duty all the twenty-four hours, without even a wink of sleep. "*Sri Rama Jayam.*"

The Goddess of Sleep did not like this. She had everyone under her power. As soon as she approached anyone he obediently went to sleep. When she stayed away they felt very miserable and begged her to be kind and come to them. Yet here was Lakshmana, never taking a nap nor even needing it. She wanted to bring him under her sway somehow or the other. So, one day, she came to him with all her winning ways. She tried to tempt him to take a nap. Lakshmana was firm and adamant. He said, "Thank you, Goddess, for your compassion. I am in *deeksha* now for fourteen years to serve my brother without relaxing. Until this period is over and we are all happily back in Ayodhya, I won't sleep a wink. *Sri Rama Jayam.*"

Hearing this firm decision the goddess had to admit her defeat and retreat. While leaving, however, she laid down a condition. "Very well. For these fourteen years I will stay away from you. But once you reach Ayodhya you must allow me to have my way. I will choose my own time to visit you and you shouldn't resist me then." Lakshmana solemnly agreed, little thinking of the consequences.

The fourteen years passed and at last the day arrived for Sri Rama's coronation. *"Sri Rama Jayam."*

At the appointed time all gathered in their respective seats in the spacious hall where the coronation was to take place. Shehnais were playing sweetly. Brahmins were chanting sacred mantras. Elderly ladies were singing auspicious songs. Young girls were offering flowers to the guests. Sri Rama and Sita were anointed king and queen. Guru Vasishtha applied the sacred tilak on their foreheads, while the elders showered auspicious *akshat* (rice used for puja) over them. Lakshmana was sitting in his seat, happy and joyous. He had eagerly waited for years to see the coronation of his beloved brother. *"Sri Rama Jayam."* Suddenly his eyes drooped down heavily and a yawn came which he could not resist... and there was a low whisper in his ears, "Ah, Lakshmana, I kept my promise for fourteen years and never approached you. Now you keep your promise and succumb to me." It was the sweet voice of the Goddess of Sleep, and Lakshmana remembered the terms of their agreement fourteen years ago. So the Goddess had come to claim her due now of all times. Lakshmana could not but laugh at her eagerness. And the laugh came from deep within him, gurgling in peals and thundering in rumbling floods. He could not stop himself. He went on roaring with uncontrollable laughter.

No need to say that his laughter was heard by all. Lakshmana was dear to all. Everybody knew the devotion with which he had served Rama in the forest. This was an occasion to smile and rejoice. Of course, Lakshmana was the first to have the right to be happy. But uproarious laughter? What was it for? It was not merely joyous laughter but mocking, teasing laughter. Whom was Lakshmana mocking? What for? There was a great hush in the assembly, and uneasiness in the air.

Sri Rama heard the laughter. He thought, "Sita was in Ravana's garden for one year. Shamelessly I brought her back and made her the queen because of my lust. Lakshmana is mocking at my infatuation." He felt injured and hurt.

Sita heard the laughter. She thought, "I was imprisoned by Ravana for one year and so have fallen. Yet because of my love of power, shamelessly I sat on the throne along with Rama as the queen. Surely, Lakshmana laughs at me for my foolish ambition." She felt ashamed and hurt.

Kaikeyi heard the laughter. She thought, "Fourteen years ago I myself sent Sri Rama to the forests, and now here I am, celebrating his installation as king. Lakshmana must be thinking that I am putting on an act and is mocking at me." She covered her eyes and shed bitter tears.

The most revered *Kula-Guru* Vasishtha heard the laughter and thought, "I fixed an auspicious day for Sri Rama's coronation as crown prince fourteen years ago, after consulting the auspicious stars. But the function never took place at all. Now again I have shamelessly fixed another auspicious day for his installation. Lakshmana must be laughing at me for this sign of foolish old age." He felt hurt and humiliated.

The citizens heard the laughter. They thought, "When Lord Rama was banished to the forests, none of us shared his difficulties and sorrows. Today we have come here to rejoice in his joy when he is in affluence. Certainly Lakshmana is mocking us for our selfish nature." They all felt ashamed of themselves and hurt.

The silence grew oppressive and unbearable while everybody sat with downcast eyes. Sri Rama looked at every one and could understand what was passing through each one's mind. He grew extremely angry with Lakshmana for throwing a dampener over the celebrations. He stood up from the throne and drew his sword, loudly demanding, "What do you mean, Lakshmana, by your mocking laughter? Whom are you mocking and for what?"

Poor Lakshmana, the cause of all this havoc, never knew what his innocent laughter had done. He was still marvelling and laughing at the mischievous ways of the Goddess of Sleep. He did not notice the silence around.

Sri Rama's thundering voice awoke him with a start from his reverie and for the first time he observed the uneasiness around him. Shrewd as he was, he at once understood the feelings all around and their cause. He stood up, at once penitent and sorrowful. Folding his palms with great humility he said, "Excuse me, my brother, for my inopportune laughter. It has nothing to do with the function. It was my sole ambition to see this day when you would be crowned as the king. *Sri Rama Jayam.* Would I laugh at anybody on this most joyous occasion?"

Then he proceeded to relate how the Goddess of Sleep kept her promise to stay away from him for fourteen years when they were in the forest, and how she suddenly visited him now, when he felt relaxed for the first time. Concluding his narration, he again begged pardon for causing pain to all by his unwitting action. "*Sri Rama Jayam.*"

When the story was heard, all felt relieved and they blamed themselves for ever having misunderstood a noble person like Lakshmana. Sri Rama came down from his throne embraced Lakshmana and warmly praised him, "O Lakshmana, it was because of your sleepless vigilance that I successfully overcame all obstacles and happily returned to Ayodhya. It was foolish of me to have ever misunderstood you. Please forgive me."

The cheerfulness was again restored and the celebrations went on as merrily as ever. *"Sri Rama Jayam."*

VYASA'S WRITER

Bhagavan Vyasa was the son of the great sage Parashara. He was the first person to write the *Vedas*. Hence he is also known as Veda Vyasa.

Vyasa had a sharp brain and a mighty intellect. At one time he worked out the idea of the entire Mahabharata in his head and then thought of writing it down. The work was colossal. Who would write it for him? Finding no answer to his problem, he sat down to meditate. He meditated on Brahma, the creator of the Universe. When Brahma appeared before him, he said, "I have thought out the entire Mahabharata. But I cannot find anyone who would be equal to the task of writing it." Brahma answered, "Direct your prayers to Ganapati. Ask him to be your scribe (writer)." So Vyasa now meditated upon Ganapati.

अजं निर्विकल्पं निराकारमेकं
निरानन्दमऽऽनन्दमद्वैतपूर्णम् ।
परं निर्गुणं निर्विशेषं निरीहं
परब्रह्मरूपं गणेशं भजेम ।।

We offer our worship to Lord Ganesha, who is Unborn, Absolute and Formless; who is beyond Bliss, and again Bliss itself. . . the One and the Infinite; who is Supreme without attributes, differentiation and desire; and who is verily the Supreme *Brahman.*

गुणातीतमानं चिदानन्दरूपं
चिदाभासकं सर्वगं ज्ञानगम्यम् ।
मुनिध्येयमाकाशरूपं परेशं
परब्रह्मरूपं गणेशं भजेम ।।

We offer our worship to Lord Ganesha, whose nature is beyond attributes; who is the embodiment of Intelligence and Bliss, the Effulgent Spirit, the All-pervading, the Goal of

Knowledge; who is the object of meditation for the sages, Formless and Omnipresent like space; and who is the Supreme Lord, the Supreme *Brahman.*

जगत्कारणं कारणज्ञानरूपं
सुरादिं सुखादिं गणेशं गणेशम् ।
जगद्व्यापिनं विश्ववन्द्यं सुरेशं ।
परब्रह्मरूपं गणेशं भजेम ।।

We offer our worship to Lord Ganesha, who is the Cause of the world, the Primal

Knowledge, the Origin of gods, the Source of Bliss, the Lord of Gunas, the Lord of heavenly hosts; who pervades the universe and is worshipped by all; who is the Lord of gods and who is verily the Supreme *Brahman*.

When Ganesha appeared before Vyasa, he said, "I want you to be my scribe. I want you to write down the Mahabharata at my dictation. Please answer my prayers."

Ganapati smiled and said, "Most gladly I will be your scribe. But I have one condition. At no point must my pen stop writing. Your dictation should be continuous."

This was a little tough, indeed. So Vyasa, after a moment's thought, said, "All right. I agree to your condition. But I, too, have a condition to make—that you will not write down anything unless you understand its meaning fully."
Ganapati agreed to this.

In between, Vyasa needed time to think out his stanzas clearly. He needed time for his bath, prayers, food and a little nap. So he would cleverly compose a few difficult stanzas and dictate them. Lord Ganesha, to fulfil his part of the bargain, had to pause and work out their meaning. Meanwhile Vyasa would get the next set of verses ready in his mind and return after his food and rest!

Thus was the great and holy book *Mahabharata* completed—written down by Lord Ganapati and dictated by the poet-sage Vyasa.

QUEEN RAMPYARI

A good king once visited the weavers' colony and entered a cottage to see for himself how they lived and worked. The king saw a girl—fair, beautiful and simple sitting in a corner. The weaver was happy that his daughter Rampyari was attracting the attention of the old king. He started extolling the glories of his daughter.

He said, "She can spin golden threads even out of hay, and she does it very very fast." When the king heard this, he said, "If this is true she shall be my daughter-in-law. Let her come with me to the palace." So saying the king departed. Poor Rampyari barely got time to pack a few things. Her father was very unhappy, but could do nothing. Rampyari prayed fervently to the Lord for help –

"Sri Ram Jai Ram Jai Jai Ram
Sri Ram Jai Ram Jai Jai Ram"

She prostrated at the feet of her parents and left for the king's palace with the officers.

The king immediately ordered a room full of hay. Rampyari was given three spinning wheels and the king commanded, "Before dawn tomorrow you must spin the entire hay into golden threads." They closed the door and went away. The poor girl wept the whole day. She could not make even an inch of golden thread out of hay. She was sure the king would punish her and her parents. All Rampyari could do was to pray.

Night fell , but she could not sleep. She had not even started spinning – and how could she? She wept... and surrendered to her Lord, chanting in her heart–

"Sri Ram Jai Ram Jai Jai Ram
Sri Ram Jai Ram Jai Jai Ram"

What was that? Was it thieves? Maybe the soldiers? Maybe the king himself had come to see her at work? Lo! Again! A soft knock? Yes....Yes.... Chanting the Lord's name for courage, the girl got up and opened the door!

What did she see? Three ugly ladies stood before her! One had big, broad feet, another had a big, hanging lower lip, and the third had a broad, ugly, big thumb. The poor girl was frightened. But the ugly ladies softly said, "We have been sent by the Lord to help you. We shall finish the work for you." The poor girl was silent and full of devotion for the Lord. Rampyari felt overwhelmed by His grace, and cried out in gratitude –

"Sri Ram Jai Ram Jai Jai Ram
Sri Ram Jai Ram Jai Jai Ram"

The three ladies worked with miraculous speed, spinning fine golden threads from the hay! By morning the entire hay was spun into golden threads. Leaving the thread with the girl, neatly laid out in reels over reels, the ugly ladies went away.

When the king saw that the hay had really been woven into golden threads, he was very surprised. He said to his ministers, "Maybe there is some trick in it. Nobody can do such a thing. Fill the room with hay and remove all these reels. Let her weave the entire hay by tomorrow morning." The guards around her room were doubled and alerted.

The king went away and the hay was brought in. The girl was again alone and in trouble, but deep within she felt a great confidence. She was sure her Ramchandraji would not desert her. She sang –

"Sri Ram Jai Ram Jai Jai Ram
Sri Ram Jai Ram Jai Jai Ram"

She ate her food, and feeling sleepy lay down and slept. The prince saw the golden thread spun by the smart girl and wanted to see her. He entered the room and saw the beautiful girl fast asleep. He thought, "Even if she won't spin so well, I will marry her!"

The Lord's grace has no end. At night again Rampyari heard the knock—*tuck-tuck-tuck*—soft, sure, determined. Now, she was not afraid. She ran and opened the door. The three smiling women were there again. They walked in, took up the work, finished it and were ready to go by dawn. The poor girl was up all night sitting in a corner, mentally chanting with devotion –

"Sri Ram Jai Ram Jai Jai Ram
Sri Ram Jai Ram Jai Jai Ram"

As the ladies were leaving, Rampyari fell at their feet, and said, "You know I am a poor, helpless girl. You have helped me for two nights. I have nothing to give you except this simple ring. Please accept it from me." The ugly women laughed. They replied, "No. We won't accept anything from you. If you want to show your gratitude, you can do one thing for us." Rampyari said, "Oh yes! I will do whatever you say."

"Now listen," said the eldest of the ugly

ladies, "tomorrow when the king sees the threads he will be convinced, and your wedding with the prince will be fixed. After that there will be a great banquet. Invite us to that as your poor, old cousins. See that we get seats close to you at the same table. That is what we want." Rampyari gladly promised this. She was ready to give even her life for these women. They went away happy.

The next day, the king saw the threads woven out of hay, laid out in reels and reels. He was beside himself with joy and admiration. The marriage was announced in a week's time. Preparations for the wedding started in earnest.

On the wedding day the three ugly ladies came. Rampyari ran to receive them and introduced them as her 'cousins'. She seated them at the banquet table. Everybody was surprised. They wondered how so beautiful a queen could have such ugly cousins!

The most curious of the guests asked one of the ugly three, why her feet were so broad. She replied, "Because I spin always." Another approached the second ugly lady and asked, "Why is your lip so large?" She replied, "By wetting the thread that I spin." A third asked the last of the ugly ones, "Why is your thumb so big?" Smiling horribly, she replied, "Because I use it to twist the threads into smooth shape."

The prince was listening to this talk. He cried out, " I will not allow my charming wife to spin hereafter." Everybody was surprised. Queen Rampyari understood and looked at her 'cousins'. They winked at her knowingly. Rampyari got up and sang, and all the court joined her in singing —

*"Sri Ram Jai Ram Jai Jai Ram
Sri Ram Jai Ram Jai Jai Ram"*.

List of Childrens Books

1. Bala Bhagavatam

2. Bala Ramayanam

3. Bala Vihar Guide I

4. Bala Vihar Guide II

5. The Balvihar Book of Picture parables

6. The Balvihar Book of Gurudev's Tales

7. The Balvihar Book of Train the Brain

8. The Balvihar Book of Prayers

9. The Balvihar Book of Jokes -1

10. The Balvihar Book of Jokes -2

11. The Balvihar Book of Hanuman Chalisa

12. Ganesha Goes to a Party